THE GOLDEN BULL OF SICILY

Frederick II
Holy Roman Emperor

Translated by: D.P. Curtin

THE GOLDEN BULL OF SICILY

Copyright @ 2022 Dalcassian Press

All rights reserved. No part of this publication may be reproduced, distributed, or transmitted in any form or by any means, including photocopying, recording, or other electronic or mechanical methods, without the prior written permission of the publisher, except in the case of brief quotations embodied in critical reviews and certain other non-commercial uses permitted by copyright law. For permission request, write to Dalcassian Press at dalcassianpublishing at gmail.com

ISBN: 979-8-8693-3571-5 (Paperback)

Library of Congress Control Number:
Author: Curtin, D.P. (1985-)

Printed by Ingram Content Group, 1 Ingram Blvd, La Vergne, Tennessee

First printing edition 2022.

THE GOLDEN BULL OF SICILY

THE GOLDEN BULL OF SICILY

Fredericus, by divine favor and clemency, elected emperor of the Romans and always august, king of Sicily, the duchy of Apulia and the principality of Capua.

Since the beauty and power of the empire has preceded our state, so that not only the dignities of other princes, but also the royal scepters are conferred by our majesty, we esteem it glorious and magnificent, that in so much of our generosity and favor to others the increase of royal dignity increases, and for this reason our eminence suffers nothing loss.

This is the reason why, observing us, the remarkable devotion which the whole nation of the Bohemians, from ancient Roman times, has shown to the government as faithfully and devoutly, and that their illustrious king Ottacharvs, from the first among other princes, specially chose us as emperor before the rest, and by persevering in our election diligently and profitably as our beloved uncle, king Philip, in pious memory, established by his privilege, after the advice of all the princes, we establish and confirm the king himself, and we approve of such a holy and worthy constitution; and we grant the kingdom of Bohemia liberally and without any exaction of money, and the usual justices of our court to him and his successors forever; desiring that whoever was chosen by them to be king should approach us or our successors, and receive the royalties in due manner. All the lands which seem to belong to

THE GOLDEN BULL OF SICILY

the aforesaid kingdom, in whatever way they have been alienated, we indulge him and his successors to possess. We grant also the right and authority to invest the bishops of his kingdom integrally to himself and to his heirs; so, however, that they themselves enjoy that liberty and security which they were wont to have from our predecessors. We decreed from our generous liberality that the aforesaid king or his heirs should not be bound to come to any of our courts, except those which we had directed to be held at Babenburg or Nuremberg, or if we had decided to hold a court at Merseburg, they themselves would be bound to do so; that if the leader of Poland should come when he was called, they themselves should provide leadership, as their predecessors, once kings of Bohemia, were wont to do; so, however, that a period of six weeks should be fixed before them for coming to the aforesaid courts; save, however, that if we or our successors happen to be crowned at Rome, we leave it to the decision of the aforesaid king Ottachar himself or his successors, whether they themselves send us three hundred men-at-arms, or pay three hundred marches.

And for the memory and strength of this constitution and confirmation of ours, we have commanded that the present privilege be communicated through the hands of Henry of Paris, our notary and faithful, to our scribe and our golden boss, signed in the year, month, and indictment.

These are the witnesses of this matter: the archbishop of Barensis; the bishop of Trent, the bishop of Basil, the bishop of Constantia, the bishop of Curia; the abbot of Augens, the abbot of St. Gall, the abbot of Wiceburg, Bertold of Nisphe, prothonotary of the royal court; count William de Chiburc, count Rudolf of Habsburg and landgrave of Alsace, counts Lodvicus and Hermannus de Froburg; count Warner of Hohenburg, Arnold the noble of Wart, Rudolf the advocate of Raprehteshiwilar, Rudolf of Ramensberg, Albert of Tanehuse the chamberlain, and many other magnates and nobles and children, by whose testimony it is evident that this privilege was confirmed.

They took place in this year, on the Sunday of the Incarnation, one thousand two hundred and twelfth, in the month of September, the fifteenth of the indictment, and the fifteenth of the reign of our lord Frederick, the most illustrious Roman emperor-elect and always august, king of Sicily.

Given in the noble city of Basel by the hands of Ulrich the vice-prothonotary, on the sixth calendar of October, happily amen.

LATIN TEXT

Fredericus, divina favente clementia Romanorum imperator electus et semper augustus, rex Sicilie, ducatus Apulie et principatus Capue.

Cum decor et potestas imperii nostrum precesserit statum, ut non solum ceterorum principum dignitates, verum etiam sceptra regalia a nostra conferantur maiestate, gloriosum reputamus ac magnificum, quod in tanto nostre largitatis beneficio et aliis crescit regie dignitatis augmentum, nec ob hoc eminentia nostra aliquod patitur detrimentum.

Inde est, quod nos attendentes preclara devotionis obsequia, que universa Boemorum gens ab antiquo tempore Romano exibuit imperio tam fideliter quam devote, et quod illustris rex eorum Ottacharvs a primo inter alios principes specialiter pre ceteris in imperatorem nos elegit et nostre electionis perseverantie diligenter et utiliter astiterit: sicut dilectus patruus noster, pie memorie rex Philippus, omnium principum habito consilio, per suum privilegium instituit, ipsum regem constituimus et confirmamus et tam sanctam et dignam constitutionem approbamus; regnumque Boemie liberaliter et absque omni pecunie exactione et consueta curie nostre iusticia sibi suisque successoribus in perpetuum concedimus; volentes, ut quicumque ab ipsis in regem electus fuerit, ad nos vel successores nostros accedat, regalia debito modo recepturus. Omnes etiam terminos, qui predicto regno attinere videntur, quocumque modo alienati sint, ei et successoribus suis possidendos indulgemus. Ius quoque et auctoritatem investiendi episcopos regni sui integraliter sibi et heredibus suis concedimus; ita tamen, quod ipsi ea gaudeant libertate et securitate, quam a nostris predecessoribus habere consueverunt. De nostre autem liberalitatis munificentia statuimus, quod illustris rex predictus vel heredes sui ad nullam curiam nostram venire teneantur, nisi quam nos apud Babenberc vel Nurenberc celebrandam indixerimus, vel si apud Merseburc curiam celebrare decreverimus, ipsi sic venire teneantur; quod si dux Polonie vocatus accesserit, ipsi sibi ducatum prestare debeant, sicut antecessores sui, quondam Boemie reges, facere consueverunt; sic tamen, ut spatium sex eddomadarum veniendi ad predictas curias eis ante prefigatur; salvo tamen, quod si nos vel successores nostros Rome coronari contigerit, ipsius predicti regis Ottachari vel successorum suorum relinquimus arbitrio, utrum ipsi trecentos armatos nobis transmittant, vel trecentas marchas persolvant.

Ad huius autem constitutionis et confirmationis nostre memoriam et robur perpetuo valiturum presens privilegium per manus Henrici de Parisius, notarii et fidelis nostri, scribi et bulla nostra aurea iussimus communiri, anno, mense et indictione subscriptis.

Huius rei testes sunt isti: archiepiscopus Barensis; episcopus Tridentinus, episcopus Basiliensis, episcopus Constantiensis, episcopus Curiensis; abbas Augensis, abbas sancti Galii, abbas de Wiceburc, Bertoldus de Nisphe regalis curie prothonotarius; comes Vlricus de Chiburc, comes Rodulfus de Habechesburc et langravius de Alsatia, comites Loduicus et Hermannus de Froburc; comes Warnerus de Hohenburc, Arnoldus nobilis de Wart, Rodulfus advocatus de Raprehteshiwilare, Rodulfus de Ramensberc, Albero de Tanehuse camerarius et alii quam plures magnates et nobiles et liberi, quorum testimonio hoc privilegium constat esse confirmatum.

Acta sunt hec anno dominice incarnationis millesimo ducentesimo duodecimo, mense septembris, quintedecime indictionis, regni vero domini nostri Frederici, illustrissimi Romanorum imperatoris electi et semper augusti, regis Sicilie, quintodecimo.

Datum in nobili civitate Basiliensi per manus Vlrici viceprothonotarii, sexto kalendas octobris, feliciter amen.

CZECH TEXT

Fridrich, z boží milosti volený císař římský a po všechny časy rozmnožitel, král Sicílie, vévoda Apulie a kníže Capue.

Poněvadž ozdoba a moc císařská předchází náš stav, že nejen hodnosti ostatních knížat, ale také královská žezla uděluje náš majestát, považujeme za slavnou a velikou věc, že v tak velikém dobrodiní naší štědrosti i jiným vzrůstá přírůstek královské důstojnosti, aniž by tím naše vznešenost trpěla nějakou újmu.

Proto my, přihlížejíce k přeslavným službám oddanosti. které veškerý lid Čechů od dávného času věrně i oddaně prokazoval císařství římskému, a že jejich jasný král Otakar od začátku mezi jinými knížaty, zvláště před ostatními, nás zvolil císařem a při naší volbě ustavičně a užitečně setrval; jako milý náš strýc, zbožné paměti král Filip, učiniv poradu se všemi knížaty, ustanovil svým privilegiem, i my jej králem ustanovujeme a potvrzujeme, a tak posvátné a důstojné ustanovení schvalujeme a České království svobodně a beze všeho vymáhání peněz i obvyklé spravedlnosti dvora našeho jemu a jeho nástupcům na věky propůjčujeme. Chtějíce, aby kdokoli od nich bude zvolen králem, k nám nebo našim nástupcům přijel a náležitým způsobem odznaky královské přijal. Také povolujeme, aby on a jeho nástupcové drželi všechny hranice, které zmíněnému království patří, ať by jakkoli byly odcizeny. Také jemu a jeho dědicům úplně povolujeme právo a moc potvrzovati biskupy jeho království; avšak tak, aby se těšili té svobodě a bezpečnosti, kterou mívali od našich předchůdců. Ustanovujeme potom z nadbytku naší štědrosti, že řečený jasný král nebo jeho dědicové nejsou povinni choditi na žádný náš sněm, než který bychom svolali do Bamberka nebo do Norimberka. Pokud bychom nařídili konat sněm v Merseburku, jen tehdy jsou povinni přijíti, jestliže kníže polský, jsa pozván, přijde a mají mu poskytnout doprovod, tak jako předchůdcové jeho, kdysi králové čeští, činívali. Avšak tak, aby jim napřed byla určena lhůta šesti neděl k příchodu ke zmíněným sněmům. S tou však výhradou, kdybychom my nebo naši nástupci byli v Římě korunováni, ponecháváme na vůli řečenému králi Otakarovi nebo jeho nástupcům, zda nám pošlou tři sta oděnců nebo zaplatí tři sta hřiven.

K trvalé paměti a moci tohoto našeho ustanovení a potvrzení poručili jsme toto privilegium napsati rukou Jindřicha z Paříže, notáře a věrného našeho, a naší zlatou bulou utvrditi, roku, měsíce a indikce níže psaných.

Této věci svědkové jsou tito: arcibiskup z Bari, biskup z Tridentu, biskup z Basileje, biskup z Kostnice, biskup z Churu; opat z Reichenau, opat ze St. Gallen, opat z Weissenburgu, Bertold z Neuffen, protonotář královského dvora; hrabě Oldřich z Kiburku, hrabě Rudolf z Habsburku a lantkrabě z Alsaska, hrabata Ludvík a Heřman z Froburku, hrabě Werner z Hohenburku, šlechtic Arnold z Wartu, fojt Rudolf z Rapperswillu, Rudolf z Ramensberku, komorník Albero z Tanenhausu a mnoho jiných velmožů a šlechticů a svobodníků. jejichž svědectvím je toto privilegium potvrzeno.

Stalo se léta od vtělení Páně tisícího dvoustého dvanáctého, v měsíci září, v patnácté indikci. skutečného království pána našeho Fridricha, nejjasnějšího zvoleného císaře římského a po všechny časy rozmnožitele říše, krále Sicílie, roku patnáctého.

Dáno ve vznešeném městě Basileji rukou místoprotonotáře Oldřicha dvacátého šestého září šťastně. Amen.

The Scriptorium Project is the work of a small group of lay people of various apostolic churches who are interested in the preservation, transmission, and translation of the works of the early and medieval church. Our efforts are to make the works of the church fathers accessible to anyone who might have an interest in Christian antiquities and the theological, philosophical, and moral writings that have become the bedrock of Western Civilization.

To-date, our releases have pulled from the Greek, Syriac, Georgian, Latin, Celtic, Ethiopian, and Coptic traditions of Christianity, and have been pulled from sundry local traditions and languages.

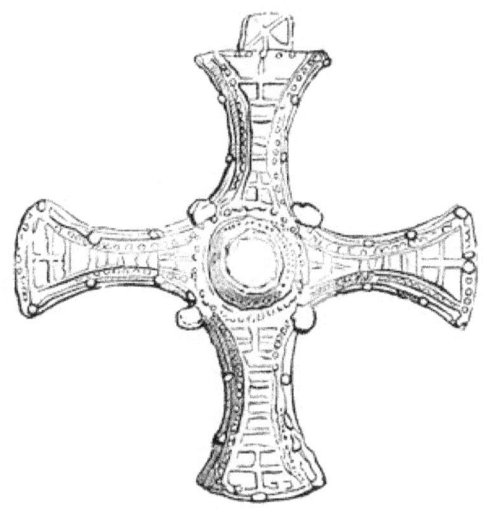

Other Selections from the Medieval German Church Series:

Passion of St. Gangolf by Hrotsvitha of Gandersheim (Oct. 2005)
Acts of the Synod of Ingelheim by Otto I, Holy Roman Emperor (Nov. 2005)
Church Documents by Louis II the German (Dec. 2005)
Imperial Edicts by Otto I, Holy Roman Emperor (Jan. 2006)
Pillars of the Slavic Church by Louis II the German (Jan. 2009)
Life of St. Bruno by Roger of Cologne (June 2009)
On the Deeds of St. Henry by Adalbold II of Utrecht (July 2010)
Letters by Gozpert of Tegernsee (Sept. 2010)
Paphnutius & Thaïs by Hrotsvitha of Gandersheim (June 2011)
Letters by Rudolf I Habsburg, Holy Roman Emperor (Dec. 2012)
About Fifteen Problems (De quindecim problematibus) by St. Albertus Magnus (Feb 2022)
The Golden Bull of Sicily by Frederick II, Holy Roman Emperor (Nov. 2022)
On Fate (De Fato) by St. Albertus Magnus (Feb 2023)

www.ingramcontent.com/pod-product-compliance
Lightning Source LLC
LaVergne TN
LVHW052049070526
838201LV00086B/5183